LIFE IN THE FAST LANE

INSIDE A
DRAG RACER

COLLIN MACARTHUR

Cavendish
Square

New York

Published in 2015 by Cavendish Square Publishing, LLC
243 5th Avenue, Suite 136, New York, NY 10016

Copyright © 2015 by Cavendish Square Publishing, LLC

First Edition

Library of Congress Cataloging-in-Publication Data
MacArthur, Collin, author.
Inside a drag racer / Collin MacArthur.
pages cm. — (Life in the fast lane)
Includes bibliographical references and index.
ISBN 978-1-62713-049-3 (hardcover) ISBN 978-1-62713-051-6 (ebook)
1. Dragsters—Juvenile literature. 2. Automobile racing—Juvenile literature. I. Title.

TL236.2.M324 2015
796.72—dc23

2014012760

Editorial Director: Dean Miller
Art Director: Jeffrey Talbot
Production Manager: Jennifer Ryder-Talbot
Production Editor: David McNamara

Packaged for Cavendish Square Publishing, LLC by BlueAppleWorks Inc.
Managing Editor: Melissa McClellan
Designer: Tibor Choleva
Photo Research: Joshua Avramson, Melissa McClellan
Copy Editor: Janice Dyer

The photographs in this book are used by permission and through the courtesy of: Cover photo by Walter G
Arce/Cal Sport Media;News.com ;p. 4 © Derek Yegan/Shutterstock.com; p. 6 top © Bruce Jenkins/Dreamstime.
com; p. 6 middle © Wisconsinart/Dreamstime.com; p. 6 bottom © Chris Curtis/Shutterstock.com; p. 8–9 ©
MCA/Universal Pictures/Photofest; p. 10, 20 inset, 20–21 © Steve Mann/Dreamstime.com; p. 12 © Phillip
Rubino /Shutterstock.com; p. 13, 22, 26, 28–29 Action Sports Photography/Shutterstock.com; p. 15 © Gary
Bydlo/Dreamstime.com; p. 16 © Redwood8/Dreamstime.com; p. 19 © Tkpphotography/Dreamstime.com; p. 25
© Josh Holmberg/Keystone Press;
p. 31 © Terry Poche /Shutterstock.com; p. 32–33 © Rozenn Leard/Dreamstime.com,
p. 35 courtesy of Shirley Muldowney; p. 36 © Derek Yegan/Shutterstock.com;
p. 38–39 © Raynald Bélanger/Dreamstime.com; p. 40 © Dreamstime.com

Printed in the United States of America

CONTENTS

Fans come to drag races to see fast cars, hear them roar, and share in the excitement.

Imagine going from complete rest to 100 miles per hour (161 km/h) in 1.2 seconds. It's almost like being on a rocket ship. The car **accelerates** so quickly that the front wheels lift off the ground. The tires struggle to **grip** the track as the car surges forward.

The stadium is packed. Fifty thousand eyes focus on a single strip of track. No one in the audience dares to look away. The sharp smell of burning rubber fills the air. Halfway through the race, the car is going 260 miles per hour (418 km/h). By the end of the race, the car is going over 333 miles per hour (536 km/h). And it's over in less than 5 seconds.

Drag racing tests the nerves. It is the motor sports' version of a sprint run— sheer speed. When dragsters burn across the track at full speed, they look like bright blurs of color. If a driver blinks or hesitates, he or she could lose the race.

Early drag racing drivers used to meet in deserts and dry lake beds to race their fixed up cars.

IN THE BEGINNING

As soon as cars became more affordable and available in the 1930s, people wanted to race them. Drag racing began in the western United States. Speed demons started by racing in California's Mojave Desert and in dry lake beds. The first drag racers also raced on two-lane roadways. Of course, back in the 1930s, Californian towns didn't have many streets. So drivers competed on flat stretches of dirt.

Drag–racing competitions were easier to participate in than other forms of racing. People didn't have to spend money on new cars. They improved the ones they already owned. Drivers fixed up their engines and transmissions so their cars would accelerate, or pick up speed, faster. They didn't need a fancy racetrack, either. They just used the longest street in town. Drivers would challenge each other to a race, and fans would line the roadway to watch.

Drivers get ready for a race on a two-lane road. Two-lane roadways often served as racetracks.

After World War II (1941–1945), drag races took place on empty military airfields or in giant parking lots. Drag racing competitions didn't require a lot of space, time, or money. Newspapers called these first drag racers **hot-rodders**. Hot-rodders raced to win, but they were also happy when a friend sped to victory and into the record books.

The idea of speed didn't just appeal to hot-rodders. It also excited people who wanted to see a good race. Many people would come to drag races.

The Start of the NHRA

One of drag racing's biggest fans was Wally Parks. Parks was a racer who lived in California. When he wasn't racing, he watched others race. In the 1940s, Parks began to worry about problems that were sneaking into his beloved sport.

Cars were becoming less safe. Explosions and spinouts were common. Some drivers, called shot-rodders, turned to thievery. They broke into garages and stole parts for their hot rods. So in 1951, Wally Parks formed a group known as the National Hot Rod

Today's dragsters have a strong steel frame
and roll bars to help protect the driver.

Association (NHRA). Thanks to the NHRA, drag racing became safer. Racers were required to wear helmets. Cars were equipped with **roll bars**. Roll bars kept drivers from getting hurt if the cars flipped. The NHRA introduced other performance standards and safety rules. This helped **legitimize** the sport, or make it more official.

Parks used NHRA membership money to award prizes and begin a championship called the Nationals. This event was held at a new spot each year so that people in different parts of the country would be exposed to the sport. Gradually, the cars' performances improved. In the early 1950s, hot–rods began to exceed 100 mph (161 km/h). Because of Wally Parks's vision, drag racing became a national hit.

Since 1969, drag racing's most **prestigious** trophy is known as the Wally Trophy in honor of NHRA founder Wally Parks. Drag racers across the country compete to win this highly respected trophy. The competitors say it represents all the hard work and dedication they put into the sport over the years. Winning it is the peak of many racers' careers.

Innovative Drag Racers

As drag racing became more popular, racing fans began to regard the drivers as celebrities. Drivers were given wild nicknames, such as Freight Train and Time Machine. One driver began calling himself The Snake. Another driver got sick of reading articles about The Snake all the time. So he nicknamed himself The Mongoose—a snake's natural enemy!

Dragsters now have rear engines. Don "Big Daddy" Garlits (at right) came up with the idea.

The first NHRA event was held in 1953 in the Los Angeles County Fairgrounds. The track is still used today. The NHRA is one of the largest motorsports organizations in the world, with 80,000 members.

The biggest drag racing hero of the 1950s was Don "Big Daddy" Garlits. He won races and broke speed records every year. But Garlits was more than just a thrilling driver. He was an **innovator**. He worked hard to

improve the design, mechanics, and safety of dragsters.

When Garlits first started drag racing, engines were placed in the front of the cars. During one race, Garlits's car engine caught fire. His foot was badly burned. But Garlits refused to give up. He designed a new dragster, placing the engine in the back. This design made dragsters safer. Rear-engine drag racers are standard today.

WHAT IS A "DRAG," ANYWAY?

We know how drag racing started. But why is it called drag racing in the first place? No one really knows for sure. Some say it's because the best place to hold racing runs was on the longest, straightest street in town. This street was often called the main drag. A few fans believe the term was borrowed from car mechanics. When drivers "drag" gears, they hold the transmission longer than normal. Other people insist it was part of a driver's challenge. ("You think your car is faster than mine? Well, let's drag it out and have a race!") The name's origin, or beginning, remains a mystery. But the name certainly has stuck.

Early drag racing cars, called "hot rods," had engines in the front. The first hot rods were most often Fords with modified chassis and engines.

Other innovations helped make this era of drag racing very exciting. For example, one racer stripped part of the frame off his car to make it lighter, and it became the first "dragster." This lighter **chassis** led to faster speeds and a new design. Also, tire companies started designing wider tires with gummy surfaces. These tires produced greater grip, or traction, on the drag strip. Again, this helped the cars go faster.

Today's dragster engines are big and powerful.

2 GOING FASTER AND FASTER

The sport of drag racing underwent major changes in the 1950s. Drivers and mechanics began to try different fuels in their hot rods. They found that, although regular gasoline worked well, other mixtures worked better. They also kept working on their cars to make them go faster. They would work for hours adjusting parts of the engine, such as the **cylinder head** or the **carburetor**, a tiny bit. Their only goal was to increase the car's speed just a little bit more.

All these differences began to separate one hot rod from the next. Eventually some cars were so much faster than others that the races weren't fair. The NHRA decided to divide hot rods into groups. This is called **classification**. Today, there are more than two hundred classes of dragsters. The three most popular are the Top Fuel, Funny Car, and Pro Stock categories. The fastest and most familiar of the three is the Top Fuel.

Top Fuel Dragsters

The shape of Top Fuel dragsters should be familiar. They are long and low to the ground. They become pointed toward the nose, like a needle, with small front wheels and large rear wheels. Top Fuel cars are shaped this way for a reason. This special shape helps them cut through the strong winds that hit them during a race. It improves their **aerodynamics**. Aerodynamics is a measure of how air affects an object's movement. If a hot rod isn't aerodynamic, wind can't flow smoothly over it, and the dragster's speed suffers.

FAST FACTS

Because dragsters run a short race, they need instant power and acceleration. Normal gasoline doesn't provide enough kick. Top Fuel dragsters use a mix of fuel made up of 90 percent nitromethane and 10 percent alcohol. This mixture gives the engines more power. Dragsters burn through this fuel very rapidly. For each 5-second race they run, Top Fuel cars guzzle a full tank of gas—15 gallons (57 L)!

Top Fuel dragsters are 25 feet (7.6 m) long and pointed like a needle to cut through the wind.

There is another reason why Top Fuel dragsters are built with that narrow, needle-like shape. An area of sticky rubber covers the center of dragstrips. This is the track's **groove**. Hot-rodders want their Top Fuel cars to stay on this groove. It is where the tires have the best traction. But the groove is only 8 feet (2.4 m) wide. By making the hot rod less than 5 feet (1.5 m) wide, there's a greater chance that the car will stay on the groove for the whole run. If the car gets off the groove while moving too fast, it will spin out of control.

Hot-rod tires look completely different depending on whether they are used in the front or in the back. The two in front are thin. They look like bicycle wheels. Their purpose is to steer. The two rear tires, called **slicks**, are completely bald. It looks as if their treads have worn off. Their purpose is to generate speed and traction.

The sidewalls, or sides, of most racecar tires tend to be hard. That's because they need to withstand a lot of pressure when they turn tight corners. But dragsters run

A race crew checks out a dragster's big back tires. The front tires (inset) are thin like bicycle tires.

an almost perfectly straight race, so they can have softer tires. The soft sidewalls of Top Fuel cars allow more of a tire's rubber to grip the track's surface at all times. This increases traction. More traction means higher speeds.

The Racetrack

Although there are two hundred classes of dragsters, all drag races are run in the same way. They take place on long **straightaways**. Straightaways are strips of track without

Star racer Tony Schumacher slows down with a parachute, which is standard on Top Fuel cars.

curves. The strips are one quarter of a mile (.4 km) long. They're different from tracks like the ones at the Indianapolis 500, which are oval and have many turns.

Drag runs begin at one end of the strip. When the light signals green, dragsters take off from a standing start. This means they begin the race at 0 miles per hour. But it takes only 1 second for Top Fuel cars to go from 0 to 100 mph (161 km/h). Races last less than 5 seconds. By the time the race is over, hot rods will have accelerated to speeds of more than 300 mph (483 km/h)!

Staying Safe

Driving Top Fuel dragsters can be dangerous. It's not unusual for hot rods to smoke or catch fire. NHRA officials work hard to make the cars as safe as possible. A metal safety cage surrounds each cockpit. The cage protects drivers from getting crushed in a crash. Inside each hot rod is a fire extinguisher system. If a fire breaks out, within seconds the system hoses down the engine and cockpit. But racers don't have to sit still and wait to be rescued. Top Fuel dragsters have escape hatches in their roofs in case drivers need to make a quick getaway.

Both Top Fuel dragsters and Funny Cars have parachutes in the rear. When the race ends, the driver pushes a button to release

FAST FACTS

All Top Fuel cars have a fixed wing at the rear. This wing is called an **airfoil**. Its job is to press the high winds into the ground. This creates a type of energy called **downforce**. Downforce keeps Top Fuel cars firmly on the track. It also helps hot-rod drivers stay in control.

the parachute. As the parachute swells with air, the dragster brakes. The quicker the dragster brakes, the less chance the car has of skidding off the strip and crashing.

Drag Racing Record Times

When it comes to speed records, fans can count on hot-rodders to deliver the goods. Here is a timeline of some smashing speeds, who set them, and when.

SPEED	WHO	WHEN
150 mph (241 km/h)	Lloyd Scott	1955
200 mph (322 km/h)	Don "Big Daddy" Garlits	1967
250 mph (402 km/h)	Don "Big Daddy" Garlits	1975
300 mph (483 km/h)	Kenny Bernstein	1992
330 mph (531 km/h)	Tony Schumacher	1999
332 mph (534 km/h)	Spencer Massey	2012

Top Fuel driver Spencer Massey displays the "The Wally" trophy after winning the Nationals in 2012.

A Funny Car looks more like a regular car than a needle-shaped Top Fuel dragster.

3 HOW DOES DRAG RACING WORK?

D rag races may be quick, but getting the cars ready to perform takes time and effort—it's a complicated process.

Elapsed Time Racing

The most popular kind of drag racing is **elapsed time**, or E.T. racing. Before a race, each hot rod makes a few trial runs. The elapsed time of each run is noted. E.T. is a measure of how long it takes for a hot rod to get to the finish line. The driver's mechanics compare all of the trial E.T.s. Then they guess what their car's E.T. will be during the competition. That guess is called a dial-in.

In some drag racing categories, when two cars compete, race officials compare the dial-ins. From this, they determine which car gets a head start. For instance, if Car A records a dial-in of 17, and Car B has a dial-in of 15, then Car A will get

a 2-second head start. If Cars A and B finish in a tie, the victory goes to Car B, because Car A didn't make up its head start.

Who Wins?

So why not just guess a really high dial-in? Say you know you can run the race in 15 seconds. Why not just dial in 18 instead, and get a huge head start?

If a dragster runs the race with a quicker E.T. than its dial-in, this is called a breakout.

The Funny Car dragsters are lining up for the running of the Four-Wide race at the Nationals.

The car loses and is disqualified if a break-out happens. So if Car A's dial-in is 19 and Car B's is 15, Car A gets a 4-second head start. But if Car A runs the race with an E.T. of 16, it loses—even if it crossed the finish line first. So drivers must make precise guesses on their dial-in times.

This is certainly a complex system. But it is used so that cars that perform at very different levels can compete in a fair contest.

Christmas Trees?

When hot-rodders set themselves up at the starting line, they stare at two columns of paired lights. These lights are nicknamed Christmas Trees. The top three pairs of amber (yellow) lights signal first. This means the race is just about to begin. Less than half a second later, the fourth pair of lights flashes on. These lights are green. They signal the start of the race.

Tension builds at every race. A driver's heartbeat goes from 120 beats per minute before the race to 205 beats per minute when the Christmas Tree shines green. Reaction time is critical. Drivers must make their moves at the instant that the amber lights dim and the green lights begin to shine.

There is one last light on the Christmas Tree—a red one. It signals that a driver's front wheels have crossed the starting line before the race has begun. If you see the red light during a drag race, it means that a driver has fouled out. It's an automatic dis-qualification, and the driver's day is done.

After two days of qualifying runs, sixteen cars are chosen as the top competitors.

When the green light comes on, a dragster starts racing so fast that it lifts off the ground.

Sunday is their day of sudden elimination. Two cars race each other. The winner moves on to the next round. The loser goes home. This process is repeated for several rounds. The last car still driving at the end of the day is crowned champion, or top eliminator.

Winning Strategies

Although runs begin and end in seconds, the contest is very much one of mental ability. Drivers must keep their concentration. At the same time, they have to be relaxed. For example, it's important to hold the wheel

Drivers focus on staying in their own lanes in a race. If they stray out, they will be disqualified.

firmly during a run. But if a driver grips it too hard, an oversteer can occur. This happens when the wheel jerks too sharply. It often results in a spinout.

Drivers need to watch the Christmas Tree closely and be ready to accelerate the instant the green light appears. The driver's reaction time is very important. The faster the driver reacts to the green light, the faster the car can leave the starting line. But the driver also has to make sure not to start too early and be disqualified.

Drivers need to stay in their own lanes as well. If they cross over into their opponent's lane, they are disqualified. Drivers also need to make sure to shift gears at the right time during the race to make the car go as fast as possible. But there are ideal times for shifting to maximize speed. They need to practice and review technical information about the car with their mechanics to make sure they are shifting at the best time.

To be at their best, drivers must keep focused on the race at hand. Top drivers suggest to simply think about getting a great start to the race. Often, thinking about winning leads to losing, and getting distracted is a sure way to fall behind your fellow competitors.

FAST FACTS

Shirley "Cha Cha" Muldowney is known as the "First Lady of Drag Racing." Muldowney started racing on the streets of Schenectady, New York. She always knew she wanted to be a drag racer. She was the first woman to receive a license from NHRA to drive a Top Fuel dragster. She won championships in 1977, 1980, and 1982. Even though she experienced four car fires during her racing career, she kept coming back for more. In 1983, Hollywood made a movie about her life story, called *Heart Like a Wheel*. She made people see that women were just as good drag racers as men. She proved that women deserve respect on the racetrack. Muldowney retired in 2003. She has been inducted into the Motorsports Hall of Fame of America and the International Motorsports Hall of Fame.

Shirley Muldowney is an icon in the field of auto racing. She proved that women drivers could win!

Festivities last all weekend at a drag race.
There's lots for fans to see and do.

4 LET'S GO TO THE RACES

Drag racing gets more popular each year. If you're interested, you can catch the excitement on TV or on the Internet. Many TV networks carry national events. However, nothing measures up to the experience of being there. You may want to visit a newly remodeled dragstrip— like the Firebird International Raceway in Phoenix, Arizona. Or check out a brand-new dragstrip, like the Ridge Motorsports Park in Shelton, Washington.

Wherever you go, your family should buy tickets in advance. And come early! Festivities last all weekend. The first days are filled with qualifying runs. This is when it's decided who will compete in the elimination rounds. Of course, Sunday is the main event. That's the day when the champion is decided.

The sport of drag racing is generally very fan-friendly. Event organizers know that not every spectator is an expert. So after big runs, an announcer will explain why a driver

won or lost. When the day is over, you can walk by the pits. There's a good chance that a hot-rodder will answer a question or sign your program. Maybe you'll even get the champion's autograph.

Junior Drag Racing

If what you see at the raceways inspires you, there may be a place for you in a hot-rod cockpit. A great place to get started is the Junior Drag Racing League (JDRL). This organization, founded in 1992, is part of the NHRA. It is geared toward giving young

Junior drivers race in cars that are half the size of a regular dragster. Kids as young as eight compete in the Junior Drag Racing League.

people a chance to race. Boys and girls of all ages can join, but to actually drive a Junior Dragster you need to be eight to seventeen years old. Today, over four thousand young people compete in the JDRL each year.

The rules of the junior circuit are quite similar to those of the professional circuit. Of course, not everything is the same. The drag strip is one eighth of a mile (0.2 km), instead of one quarter of a mile (0.4 km). The cars are half the size of regular drag racing cars. Junior dragsters can reach

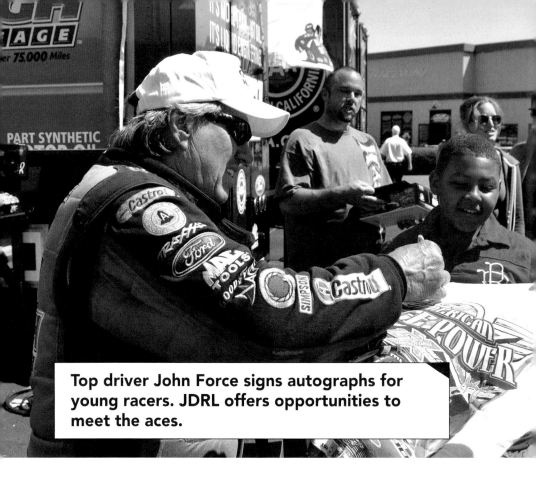

Top driver John Force signs autographs for
young racers. JDRL offers opportunities to
meet the aces.

speeds of 85 mph (137 km/h). Top drivers
run the strip in less than 8 seconds. Drivers
as young as 8 years of age can run the strip
in under 13 seconds. As in the pro categories, JDRL racing is open to everyone. It is
divided into age groups, and boys and girls
race one another. In fact, one out of every
three JDRL drivers is a girl.

JDRL is a great program to be a part of.
Members have a lot of fun. But there is

some serious competition, too. The racing year concludes with two Conference Finals. One is held on each coast of the United States. Winners receive thousands of dollars in scholarship money.

Junior drag racing is becoming more and more popular. Many members of the JDRL have gone on to successful careers in the NHRA. They use the skills they learned racing in the JDRL to compete and win in "big car" programs.

It's exciting to be a part of hot-rod action. With lots of practice, maybe you too can race into the record books!

FAST FACTS

A Junior Dragster costs about $4,000 to $5,000. Other costs include equipment, safety gear, a trailer to transport the vehicle, and maintenance. Safety is very important for the JDRL. All racers need to wear a helmet, neck collar, arm restraints, seat belts, protective clothing, and gloves. About 130 tracks in North America have JDRL programs. Junior drag racing is most popular in California, Texas, and Florida.

accelerate: to pick up speed

aerodynamics: a measure of how air affects an object's movement

airfoil: a fixed wing that is mounted on the rear of all Top Fuel cars

carburetor: the part of a car's engine that mixes air with fuel

chassis: the supporting frame of a car

classification: a system of grouping hot rods

cylinder head: part of a car's engine against which the piston compresses the contents of the cylinder

downforce: a type of energy that pushes objects toward the ground

elapsed time (E.T.): the measure of how long it takes for a hot rod to get to the finish line

WORDS TO KNOW

grip: to hold firmly

groove: an area of sticky rubber that covers the center of dragstrips

hot-rodders: the nickname given to the very first drag racers

innovator: a person who does something in a new way

legitimize: to make something more official

prestigious: important, distinguished, celebrated

roll bar: a safety feature that prevents drivers from getting crushed if their cars flip

slicks: the rear tires of a dragster

straightaways: long strips of track that do not have curves

FURTHER READING

Books

Drag Racing
Lori Polydoros
Mankato, MN
Capstone Press
2013

Junior Stock: Drag Racing
the Family Sedan
Doug Boyce
North Branch, MN
CarTech
2012

Smokin' Dragsters and Funny Cars
Jim Gigliotti
Berkeley Heights, NJ
Enslow Publishing
2013

RESOURCES

Websites

America on the Move
amhistory.si.edu/onthemove/themes/
story_66_4.html
This site explains the history of drag racing, and even compares it to other racing including NASCAR and Indy.

DragRaceCanada
dragracecanada.com
This site features profiles, schedules, and photos.

National Electric Drag Racing Association
www.nedra.com
The National Electric Drag Racing Association (NEDRA) aims to increase public awareness of electric vehicle performance and to encourage advances in electric vehicle technology.

Organizations

International Hot Rod Association
www.ihra.com
Official site of the International Hot Rod
Association. Includes information about
staff, sponsors, drivers, and member tracks.
Provides schedules of National, Divisional,
and Junior Dragster events.

National Hot Rod Association
www.nhra.com
Official site of the National Hot Rod
Association. Includes information about
drivers, events, and current racing news.
Also provides details about the Junior
Drag Racing League.

Page numbers in purple are images.

aerodynamics, 18
airfoil, 23

breakout, 28, 29

chassis, 15
Christmas Tree(s), 30, 32
classification, 17
conference finals, 41

dial-in, 27–29
disqualified, 29, 32, 33
downforce, 23

elapsed time (E.T.), 27–29
engine, 7, 12, 14, 15, 16, 17, 18, 23

Force, John, 40
Funny Car(s), 17, 23, 26, 28–29

Garlits, Don, 12, 13, 14, 24
grip, 5, 15, 21
groove, 19

hot-rodders, 8, 19, 24, 30, 38
hot-rods, 11,15, 20, 23, 38, 41

Junior Drag Racing League (JDRL), 38, 39, 40, 41

Massey, Spencer, 24, 25
Muldowney, Shirley "Cha Cha", 34, 35

About the Author

Collin MacArthur is a former automotive engineer with a master's degree in mechanical engineering. Today, Collin works as a freelance automotive interest writer. He lives in Florida with his wife, son, and dog.